I0163999

Michael B. Mukasey

Attorney General of the United States (2007-2009)

not a crime, an act of war

UNDERSTANDING THE THREAT OF 'CIVILIZATION JIHAD'

Remarks from the Center for Security Policy

2012 **Freedom Flame Award** in New York City

with an introduction by **Andrew C. McCarthy**

CENTER FOR SECURITY POLICY PRESS

Copyright © 2012 Center for Security Policy

Not A Crime, An Act of War:
Understanding the Threat of 'Civilization Jihad'
is a monograph published in the United States by the
Center for Security Policy Press,
a division of the Center for Security Policy.

THE CENTER FOR SECURITY POLICY
1901 Pennsylvania Avenue, Suite 201 Washington, DC 20006
Phone: (202) 835-9077 Email: info@securefreedom.org
For more information, please see securefreedom.org

Book design by David Reaboi.

CONTENTS

The Center for Security Policy's FREEDOM FLAME AWARD recognizes individuals who have exemplified the ideals of freedom, democracy, economic opportunity and international strength to which the Center for Security Policy is committed. The Award acknowledges the past contributions of its recipients while serving as a reminder that the goals for which they have worked so valiantly require the continuing, unflagging efforts of those who follow in their footsteps.

The award—a breathtaking crystal flame—is presented to the recipient at an elegant dinner hosted by the Center's Regents in New York City and attended by the Center's National Security Advisory Council, friends and sponsors.

RECIPIENTS OF THE FREEDOM FLAME AWARD

2012—Michael B. Mukasey

2011—John Lehman

2010—'THE MANHATTAN SEVEN'
Amanda Bowman, Tim Brown, Debra Burlingame, Aaron Harison,
Andrew C. McCarthy, Beth Gilinsky and Sgt. Tim Sumner

2009—Dr. Herb London

2008—James R. Woolsey

2007—New York City Police Commissioner Ray Kelly

2006—John Bolton

2005—Richard Perle

2004—Lawrence and Susan Kadish

2002—Senator Fred Thompson

1998—Jeane Kirkpatrick (Casey Medal of Honor)

1997—Edwin Meese III (Casey Medal of Honor)

1996—William J. Casey

1994—Robert H. Krieble

1993—Dr. Albert Wohlstetter

1992—Margaret Thatcher

On Tuesday May 22, 2012 at the Union League Club in New York City, the Center for Security Policy bestowed the 2012 FREEDOM FLAME AWARD to the Honorable Michael B. Mukasey, former Attorney General of the United States.

Mr. Mukasey's myriad accomplishments in American jurisprudence and law enforcement epitomize the commitment to freedom and the practice of "peace through strength" that the FREEDOM FLAME was created to recognize. Mr. Mukasey served from 2007 to 2009 as the eighty-first U.S. Attorney General following his appointment to that position by President George W. Bush. From 1988 to 2006, he was a federal judge in the Southern District of New York, becoming that court's Chief Judge in 2000.

Michael Mukasey rendered a singular public service as the presiding judge in the successful prosecution of Omar Abdel Rahman (the "Blind Sheik") and nine other co-conspirators convicted of the first attack on the World Trade Center in 1993.

The prosecutor in that same case, Andrew C. McCarthy, had the honor of introducing Judge Mukasey. Subsequent to the trial and to his time as an Assistant United States Attorney for the Southern District of New

York, Mr. McCarthy has become one of America's insightful writers on national security and Constitutional issues; his new book, *Spring Fever: The Illusion of Islamic Democracy*, addresses many of the points he made in paying tribute to Mr. Mukasey.

Mr. Mukasey's FREEDOM FLAME acceptance speech that night was an eloquent assessment of the threat from the doctrine of jihadist Islam from the 1993 World Trade Center attacks to the present day, providing a systematic analysis of the enemy's ideology.

Frank J. Gaffney, Jr., the Center for Security Policy's President noted that "Judge Mukasey's acceptance remarks provided a characteristically thoughtful, articulate and compelling indictment of shariah law and the Muslim Brotherhood—and those in the U.S. government who are wittingly or unwittingly enabling their insinuation into this country."

We at the Center believe future readers will find much wisdom in Mr. Mukasey's words that night in New York City; his remarks—and those of Mr. McCarthy, introducing him—form this monograph.

ANDREW C. MCCARTHY

It is not often enough that I get to salute not one but two of my favorite people. But tonight, I want to embrace that opportunity.

There is no one in America who fights more relentlessly, passionately, and effectively in the cause of freedom than Frank Gaffney. Do you care about liberty, and about the defining principles of the West—equality, freedom of conscience, freedom of expression, peace through the strength of both our culture and our armed forces? If you do, you owe a great debt of gratitude to Frank, and to the bulwark he has made of the Center for Security Policy.

We don't say "thank you" nearly often enough. So tonight, I want to make sure that we all say "thank you" for all Frank does for our country. Frank, we can never repay you, but we honor you, and we are forever grateful for your patriotism.

Next, I'd like to say a few words about my friend Michael Mukasey, who will always be Judge Mukasey to me—not just because that is how I first came to know him, but because he remains the model of what we want our judges to be.

When it comes to the notion of treating international terrorism—violent jihadism—as a law enforcement matter, there are many bad things that can be said. I know, because I've said all of them. And I've evidently said them so notoriously that, just last week, the thoughtful progressives at Salon magazine anointed me the leader of the alleged "Islamophobe" faction of the American conservative movement.

You can really tell that our movement badly needs an "Arab Spring." Not only do we not have one of those nice sharia constitutions that the State Department writes for all its favorite new, er, "democracies"—those shining cities on a hill where people are put on capital trial for what they think and what they say. We "Islamophobes" haven't even had a popular election.

You can tell we haven't had an election because—despite the fact that Salon claims the "Islamophobes" include such luminaries as John Bolton, Michele Bachmann, and, yes, Frank Gaffney—somehow, I've ended up in charge. Some leader, right? The Obama administration has been quick to point out that even those lovable, "largely secular" moderates from the Muslim Brotherhood now have more democratic legitimacy than I do!

But let's go back to the matter of treating the jihad against America as a crime problem rather than a national defense challenge. There is one very good argument in favor of using the courts—a hugely significant argument. It is this: Juries represent the common sense and the values of American life.

William F. Buckley Jr., the legendary pioneer of the modern conservative movement and founder of National Review, famously said he'd "rather entrust the government of the United States to the first 400 people listed in the Boston telephone directory than to the faculty of Harvard University."

Well, now that we've spent nearly four years being governed by the faculty of Harvard University, we can see that the pioneer has been vindicated, yet again.

We can also see that the American people would be a lot better protected if national security were designed by the twelve New Yorkers who sat in Michael Mukasey's courtroom for nine months than by, say, an intelligence community that thinks reaching out to Taliban "moderates" is the way to fix Afghanistan; or by a Justice Department that thinks reaching out to Muslim Brotherhood "moderates" is the way to fix American counterterrorism; or by a military brass that can't see its way to a single mention of the words "jihad" or "Islam" in its 75-page report on the Fort Hood massacre—the worst terrorist atrocity in this country since 9/11, a mass-murder that claimed the lives of twice as many Americans as were killed in the 1993 World Trade Center bombing.

A remarkable thing about juries—something that shouldn't be remarkable, but is—is that they tend to take their oath very seriously. They do not decide cases based on bigotry or hysteria. They decide cases based only on the evidence, and with fidelity to the law as the judge explains it to them.

Another remarkable unremarkable thing is that jurors, being ordinary Americans, tend to be rational. Juries will not convict people of serious crimes absent being convinced that they really did what they are accused of doing. That means a prosecutor has to be able to prove not only what a defendant has done, but why he has done it.

No narrative is complete, compelling, or true unless we learn a person's motivation for the things he has done. And no national security strategy can be competent or successful unless we learn what motivates our enemies to act—not so we can understand them better, as if this were some pedantic sociology project. We need to know what motivates our enemies so we can stop them, discredit them, and defeat them.

As you've heard, in the early-to-mid 1990s, I had the privilege of leading the government's prosecution against the Blind Sheikh—the terrorism case tried by Judge Mukasey. Back in those days, much like today, we had administration spokesmen, Justice Department law-yers, and intelligence community officials spouting the CAIR-certified, Muslim Brotherhood-approved, Idiot's Guide to Islam: "Religion of Peace," period, full stop, end of story.

But there is a big difference between then and now. Back in 1995, no matter what was being said in Washing-ton, in the academy, or in the media, a trial was still a trial. There was no jihad against information.

In the four corners of Judge Mukasey's courtroom, it was not only permitted but required to tell the truth.

We got to prove that there were commands to warfare against non-Muslims in Islamic scripture; that those commands were accurately conveyed by renowned scholars of Islam; and that believing Muslims were animated to commit atrocious acts under this profound influence.

Don't get me wrong. No one believed or suggested that Islamic supremacism was the only interpretation of Islam. Nor did anyone contend that all Muslims wanted to live under, much less impose, a fundamentalist construction of sharia—Islam's totalitarian framework for society. Indeed, our case could not have been proved had it not been for the pro-American patriotism of a number of Muslims who helped us infiltrate the terror cells and present a convincing case to the jury.

But it is simply a fact that we have enemies who seek to destroy the West. They are catalyzed by an ideology that is knowable. That ideology, Islamic supremacism, is derived from an interpretation of Islam that is a lot more mainstream than we would like to believe. In point of fact, it is the dominant Islam of the Middle East.

I always think the simplest way to look at it is to look at the Blind Sheikh himself. Omar Abdel Rahman was utterly incapable of performing any forcible action that would be useful to a terrorist organization. Blind from childhood and beset by various other maladies, he could not build a bomb, hijack a plane, plant an IED, or carry out an assassination. Yet, he wasn't just in the terrorist organization; he was its unquestioned leader. And unlike the imaginary "Islamophobe" faction of the American conservative movement that I supposedly lead, this was an organization that actually exists.

What qualified the Blind Sheikh to be the leader? I assure you, it wasn't charisma and good looks. The Blind Sheikh is a doctor of Islamic jurisprudence graduated from al-Azhar University in Cairo, the center of Sunni Islamic learning since the 10th Century. He is a globally recognized authority on sharia. He was able to lead our enemies because he was, indisputably, a master of their ideology.

In 1995, we were able to prove that in a court of law, solely because we had a judge who was dedicated to the rule of law—a judge who was determined that the case would be decided based not on fear or favor, but based on the facts, wherever they took us.

Judge Mukasey understood the law, and he understood that what makes America exceptional is Americans. He knew that a jury of New Yorkers, in their American sense of justice, would want to know not only what happened, but why. He knew that this was not only what common sense required, but what American law demanded.

Because of that, we not only have a dozen jihadists who were quite deservedly convicted and sentenced to long prison terms. We also have what remains the most comprehensive and accurate historical record of who our enemies are, what they want to do to us, and why.

That should not be the case. Obviously, all of us who were involved in the Blind Sheikh trial are proud to have played our parts in our nation's response when the global jihad first turned its attention to our homeland. But let's face it, almost 20 years have gone by. Yes, that means I look worse. But with two additional decades to gather intelligence and study our enemies, our country's security should look a lot better.

It doesn't. Today, we still face enemies who want to destroy us, but they are aided and abetted by people in and out of government who throw sand in our eyes: who want you to believe that the real threat to America comes not from Islamic supremacism, but from the people who are trying to expose Islamic supremacism—to alert their fellow Americans to the dangers imperiling our way of life.

Some of these people are well-meaning but foolish. Some of them, though, know exactly what they are doing. While they don't endorse terrorist methods, they do sympathize with the Islamist indictment against the United States—the old "blame America first" crowd that lays all the world's ills at our doorstep. Except ... it is not just the "blame America first" crowd. They're on the political Left. The effort to blind us to the threat, to slander as "Islamophobia" the advocacy of sound national security measures and the protection of Western institutions, has spread its tentacles into conservative circles as well.

National security should not be a conservative or liberal issue. Preserving our liberties ought to be a priority for the vast majority of Americans. Protecting our constitutional norms from sharia incursions ought to be a nonpartisan imperative.

Judge Mukasey has served America that way for his entire career. It is the light that he carried with him from the federal bench to the Justice Department, where his tenure as Attorney General was distinguished, honorable, and altogether too short.

But though it is always possible that I'm being parochial, I will always see his greatest contribution to our national security—yesterday, today and tomorrow—this way: By following the law faithfully, he ensured that history would fairly and accurately record the ideology of our enemies—not only what they did, but why they did it. Neither political correctness nor willful blindness can efface that record.

As his admiring friend, and as a proud past recipient of this award, it is my great pleasure and privilege to introduce our 2012 Freedom Flame honoree, Attorney General Michael Mukasey.

NOT A CRIME, AN ACT OF WAR

UNDERSTANDING THE THREAT OF 'CIVILIZATION JIHAD'

MICHAEL B. MUKASEY

Firtst, I want to thank my good friend Andy McCarthy for that lavish introduction. It's obvious from that introduction that he is my good friend.

I want to thank Frank Gaffney also for his kind words and also for the work that he and the Center for Security Policy do day in and day out, year in and year out, to keep before a sometimes unwilling audience the threats to the security of this country and to present a forum for developing the most effective ways to combat those threats. I would actually describe it as thankless work, but occasionally, it does elicit tributes. One of which was alluded to by Andy. Even though they may be unintentional.

About a week ago, a publication with the sophisticated moniker, *Salon*, included one of these inadvertent tributes to Frank. *Salon* hosts a variety of left-wing bloggers who would otherwise have to look to their own devices in order to get their stuff out. But it included, on May 16th, a report by *Salon*'s foreign policy correspondent to the effect that there was a struggle going on inside the conservative movement for the ear of Mitt Romney on how to deal with the Arab Spring in general, and with the

Muslim Brotherhood in particular: a struggle between what the author calls the neocons—which includes such people as Senators Lindsay Graham and John McCain—who, if you really think about it, are neither particularly *neo* nor particularly *con*—and what the author labels the "Islamophobes." Their ranks are, as you heard, are said to be led by Andy McCarthy and are said to include Frank Gaffney.

Now I kind of resent that article, because I didn't make the cut. Although I think it's possible that I'm on the wait list. As they say on the Harvard faculty. And who knows? Maybe tonight's award will get me a varsity spot.

I think what Andy and Frank and others have done to earn their prominence on this list of so-called "Islamophobes"—by the way, a phobia is an irrational fear of something and the term "Islamophobia" is inaccurate in two respects when applied to Frank and Andy. First, because that fear has nothing to do with Islam, but rather with Islamism. And it is anything but irrational.

What they have done to earn membership on that list to call attention to the fact that more than ten years after 9/11 and in fact more than sixty years after one of the earliest Islamists declared that our society was incompatible with his religion, more than twenty years since the first act of violence in this country traceable to that movement, and more than fifteen years after Osama bin Laden made specific what was already apparent by declaring that he and others like-minded were at war with us, we still seem to grapple with what it is that we're dealing with.

Now, in a sense, we are constitutionally ill-equipped to deal with that, and here I mean constitutionally, in two senses. Both our written Constitution and in our national DNA. Perhaps because of bitter experience with the role of religion in public life in the 17th and 18th Centuries, our Constitution in its very body, not just in the celebrated Bill of Rights, in Article 6 bars any religious test as a qualification for any public office. And then of course there's the establishment clause of the First Amendment which, as it is currently interpreted, reads religion out of the public square to the point where even a prayer at any official school function, be it a graduation or a football game, is forbidden.

We tend to think of religion, if we think about it at all, as only one aspect of a person's life. And a private aspect at that. So in a sense, it's natural for a people who live in such an atmosphere not to be on the lookout for attack from others to whom religion is not simply a part of life or even a way of life but is life itself. And a life in which religion has a heavy political component. But that's where the attack is coming from. And 9/11 was certainly not the beginning. Actually, as a matter of history, Islamism insofar as it holds this country in a sort of weird combination of awe and contempt, has been incubating for about as long as we knew about the other two -isms that we successfully beat back in the last century, Fascism and communism.

As a movement, distinct from the religion of Islam itself—and again, that's the sense in which I'm using it in these remarks—Islamism traces back to Egypt in the 1920s. When the loosely organized Muslim Brotherhood was established by a man named Hassan al-Banna, a primary school teacher and later an admirer of Adolf Hitler. Al-Banna founded the Muslim Brotherhood as a reaction to the modernizing influence of Kemal Ataturk who had dismantled the shell of what was left of the Muslim caliphate in Turkey, had banned fezzes and headscarves and dragged his country by the lapels and it had to be the lapels because men were barred from wearing robes, into the 20th Century.

Al-Banna's principal disciple was also an educator, a bureaucrat in the education department of the Egyptian government named Sayid Qutb, who caused enough trouble in Egypt to get himself awarded a traveling fellowship in 1948—the year al-Banna was killed in violence that was generated by the Muslim Brotherhood. That fellowship was intended to have the benign effect of getting him out of the country, and it did have that effect. But regrettably for us, he chose to travel to the United States, in particular to Greeley, Colorado.

Now I think it would probably be hard to imagine a more sedate place than post-World War II Greeley, Colorado. But for Sayid Qutb, it was Sodom and Gomorrah. He hated everything that he saw. American haircuts, enthusiasm for sports, jazz, what he called—and these are his words—"the animal-like mixing of the sexes, even in church." His conclusion was that Americans were, as he put it, "numb to faith and art, faith and religion, faith and spiritual values altogether."

Qutb went back to Egypt, quit the civil service, joined Hasan al-Banna's Muslim Brotherhood. Qutb and the Muslim Brotherhood continued to agitate for a return to fundamentalist Islam so much so that he was tried for conspiracy against the government and was hanged in Egypt in 1966.

At that time, many members of the Brotherhood fled to Saudi Arabia, where they found refuge and ideological sustenance. Qutb's brother was among those who fled and taught the doctrine in Saudi Arabia. Among his students were Ayman al-Zawahiri, an Egyptian who would later become a leading al-Qaeda ideologist. And a then-obscure Osama bin Laden, the pampered child of one of the richest construction families in the country. And the rest, as they say, is history.

That history did not come to these shores on September 11, 2001. Or even on February 26, 1993, when a truck bomb went off in the basement of the World Trade Center—killing six people, wounding hundreds, and causing millions of dollars in damage that would eventually become known as the first World Trade Center bombing. Rather, it came at the latest in the 1980s, when a couple of FBI agents spotted a group of men taking what looked like particularly aggressive target practice at a shooting range out on Long Island in Calverton. When the agents approached, they were accused of what we now call, "racial profiling" and backed off.

In November, 1990, one of the men participating in that target practice, El Sayyid Nosair, would assassinate a right-wing Israeli politician named Meir Kahane after Kahane finished delivering a speech in the ballroom of a hotel here in Manhattan. The case was treated by the Manhattan DA as the lone act of a lone gunman.

When the 1993 World Trade Center bombers demanded that Nosair be freed from jail, it became apparent that the Kahane assassination was not the lone act of a lone gunman. In fact, when authorities reviewed the amateur video of Kahane's speech the night that he was killed, they discovered that one of those 1993 bombers had been in the hall when Kahane was shot. Further investigation disclosed that another was driving what was supposed to be Nosair's getaway vehicle on that night in 1990 when Kahane was shot. When they retrieved from a warehouse materials that had been seized from Nosair's apartment but had gone unexamined, they saw that it included documents that called for the destruction of Western Civilization by toppling tall buildings.

The man who served as the spiritual adviser to Nosair and to the 1993 Trade Center bombers and who had issued the fatwa that resulted in the assassination in 1981 of Anwar Sadat, Omar Abdel-Rahman (the so-called, "Blind Sheik")—who later would issue from jail the fatwa that authorized the 9/11 attack—was tried before me, along with Nosair and several others. They were convicted for participating in a conspiracy to conduct a war of urban terror against this country that included the Kahane murder, the first Trade Center bombing, a plot to blow up other landmarks around New York, and to assassinate Hosni Mubarak when he visited the United Nations.

The list of unindicted co-conspirators in that case included Osama bin Laden, that pampered rich kid who had studied at the knee of Sayid Qutb's brother in Saudi Arabia. All of this was treated as a series of crimes. Unconventional crimes, maybe, but merely crimes.

In 1996 and again in 1998, Osama bin Laden declared that he and his cohorts were at war with the United States—a declaration that got little serious attention at the time. In 1998, our embassies in Nairobi, Kenya and Dar al Salaam, Tanzania were almost simultaneously bombed; again, the criminal law was invoked with the usual mantra of, "bring them to justice." This time, an indictment actually named bin Laden as a defendant. Apparently, he was unimpressed, or at least undeterred; in 2000, his group, al-Qaeda, bombed the *USS Cole* in Aden, killing sixteen US sailors and would have carried out the bombing of another naval vessel, the *USS The Sullivans*, but for the fact that the barge carrying the explosives was overloaded and sank.

And then of course came September 11th, 2001. And to the call, "bring them to justice" was added the call, "bring justice to them." We were told finally that we were at war, which was more than fifty years after Sayid Qutb had determined that Islamists would have to make war on us, about fifteen years after Islamists made it clear that they were training for war with us, and five years after Osama bin Laden made it official with a declaration of war.

If Islamism was simply about folks who wanted to blow up things and people, that would be bad enough; but it might be something that we could deal with. After all, we have an intelligence network that sometimes, although not always, detects our enemies. And a robust military. But the violence is not the ultimate end; it's simply a means to that end. To focus on the violence and refuse to examine the goal of the violence is like going to a play and focusing on the props rather than on the story. The story—the end meant to be served by the means of the violence—is the imposition of shariah, which is a comprehensive framework that has spiritual aspects to be sure, but is supposed to regulate all behavior (economic, social, legal, military, and political) because it is all-encompassing and lays claim to being divinely inspired. It regards the notion that people can determine the rules that govern any aspect of their lives, either themselves or through elected representatives, as anathema. As sacrilege. Which is to say, shariah is totalitarian and profoundly anti-democratic.

Hints of the comprehensive framework of shariah come peeking through even in prosecutions and episodes of support for violence that have been the subject of prosecution in civilian courts of this country. In the terrorism financing trial of an entity called the Holy Land Foundation in 2008, there was introduced into evidence a document entitled, *Explanatory Memorandum on the General Strategic Goal of the Group*. "The group" apparently refers to the Muslim Brotherhood in America.

The document was written in 1991 by a senior Hamas leader in the United States. And it explains that the "Islamic Movement" is what the memo refers to as a "settlement process" to establish itself in the United States and once established to pursue a "civilization-jihadist" mission led by the Muslim Brotherhood. What the author Robert Spencer has described, I think aptly, as stealth jihad. The document itself describes what it calls the "civilization-jihadist" process as "a kind of grand jihad in eliminating and destroying the Western Civilization from within and sabotaging its miserable house by their hands and the hands of the believers so that it is eliminated and God's religion is made victorious over all other religions."

That is to say, "God's religion is made victorious" through the implementation of shariah. The law of the land within what is referred to as the *Dar al-Islam* or the home or realm of Islam. That is not, by the way, simply Muslim countries; it's anyplace where Muslims can and do exercise control or ever have. And so in some neighborhoods in European cities where Muslims exercise control—notably in France, somewhat in England, and even in Sweden—shariah is practiced and enforced in contravention and with the suppression of local law, with the result that some of those neighborhoods have become no-go zones for police and firefighters unless they have secured the explicit permission of local enforcers. Imposing shariah on the *Dar al-Harb*, which is the abode of war, or the places where shariah is not fully implemented, is the goal of jihad.

Now all of this is readily accessible, among other places, in a volume called *Reliance of the Traveler*, which is actually endorsed for its accuracy by al-Azhar University, about which you heard a moment ago. It is located in Cairo, and is a seat of learning founded in 975 AD. Al-Azhar University is the institution that gave us Omar Abdul-Rahman, the cleric tried before me, who was the spiritual authority behind the Sadat and Kahane assassinations and both the first World Trade Center bombing and the 9/11 attack.

Are there, then, no moderate Muslims? None who are willing to live in peace, long term, with their neighbors? Of course there are. Millions reside among us in the United States as loyal Americans, and millions more reside around the world. There are even places where they are in power—notably in Indonesia, which is the most populous Muslim country in the world. Some simply disregard the requirements of shariah and, to that extent, I guess they're not so much reformists as unobservant. But a brave few are actually struggling to create within their religion a theoretical and doctrinal basis for combating supremacist Islam. They include, in the United States, Dr. Zuhdi Jasser, who heads the American Islamic Forum for Democracy. He is about to publish a book called *The Battle For The Soul of Islam,* a riveting account of both his views and his personal struggle. Dr. Jasser is, by the way, not only a medical doctor, but also a former lieutenant commander in the United States Navy.

At Princeton's James Madison Program, an Australian academic, Abdullah Saeed, recently delivered a lecture arguing that there are ways in which one can use passages in the Koran and episodes in the life of Muhammad so as to oppose classical shariah. The lecture is published in the November, 2011 issue of *First Things* under the title, "The Islamic Case For Religious Liberty." But the regrettable part of that story is that *First Things*—as I'm sure many of you know—is a Catholic, not a Muslim, publication.

Make no mistake: as numerous as they may be among those who pronounce doctrine, the moderates are the distinct and weaker minority. The majority view was stated succinctly by a political leader lately prominent on the world stage. He said that the term, "moderate Islam" is, "ugly and offensive." He said that, "there is no moderate or immoderate Islam. Islam is Islam. That's it." That politician is Recep Tayyip Erdoğan, Prime Minister of the increasingly powerful and influential Muslim nation of Turkey.

And what of the vaunted Arab Spring? What indeed? As events unfolded in Tahrir Square, we in the United States saw lots of coverage about how the driving forces of the revolution relied on Twitter and Facebook, but no so much coverage of the public rape of a CBS journalist in Tahrir Square to shouts of *Allahu Akbar*. And even less coverage of the emergence of the Sinai Peninsula as a refuge for Hamas-trained terrorists who travel regularly from Gaza, and who launch attacks that kill Israelis.

There was, I think, virtually no coverage at all of the return to Egypt of Sheik Yusuf al-Qaradawi, who had been exiled from the country by Hosni Mubarak and who delivered a triumphant sermon in Tahrir Square upon his return. Qaradawi is praised in many quarters in the West as a liberal and a reformer who, among other things, stood up for women's rights. And so he did, even to the point of issuing a fatwa authorizing women to participate in suicide bombings.

In Tunisia, Islamists are in control. Their leader, Rashid Ghannouchi, like Qaradawi, recently returned from exile to lead his party. Barely five years ago, he called for the hanging of two Tunisian intellectuals, one a woman, who were too vigorous for his tastes in their support of women's rights. But even a member of *The Wall Street Journal* editorial staff in a column assured us that Ghannouchi is a new breed of Islamist with a sense of irony and a sense of humor. Ghannouchi even assured the *Journal* editor that he would not seek to ban alcohol in Tunisia, because it's well-known that alcohol is consumed privately, and he recalled that the United States had an unpleasant experience when it tried that experiment several decades ago with Prohibition. Quite and ironist and a humorist—and, apparently, the spiritual successor to that parade of Soviet premiers, back in the 1970s who, we were told, as each one of them took power when his predecessor died, that he was "a man of peace" because, after all, he drank scotch and listened to jazz.

But isn't what's happening in Egypt and in Tunisia and in Turkey a manifestation of democracy? And aren't we duty-bound to support it because we stand for democracy? The answer to the first part of that question, as that great 'Islamophobe' Andy McCarthy has astutely pointed out, is that that depends on what you mean by democracy.

If you mean, by democracy, not only a process of majority rule but also an underlying culture that includes protection of minority rights, then, yes. But if you mean simply majority rule with no such underlying cultural tolerance, then what is happening in Egypt and Tunisia and Turkey is not democracy—and no, we are under no obligation to support that. As President Erdoğan put it, to Islamists, "democracy is just the train we board to reach our destination." The destination, obviously, is Islamist rule. And we have no obligation to support that.

Why is it important in the struggle we are in that we understand all this?

In past conflicts, it might not always have been self-evident hat we had to understand what our enemies were about. Perhaps it was not necessary, when we fought the Axis powers in Germany and Japan, to understand all the ins and outs of Nazism and fascism and the military culture of the Shinto religion; we could simply blast those countries to smithereens—as we in fact did—because the evil had its home base there.

It was much more necessary to understand the enemy when we fought communism, as Whittaker Chambers taught us. Although the threat was centered principally in the Soviet Union, it was not simply that nation but its militant ideology that we were struggling with. Chambers prefaces his excellent book *Witness* with a preface that consists of a letter to his children; in it, he explains why he went through what he did in order to expose communism for what it was, so that they could understand why he had broken with communism and, in the process, had exposed himself and them to a life of torment.

Chambers points out that communism, at its root, offered the same promise as was offered by the serpent in Eden: that "you shall be as gods." Communism dreamed of a world without God, who would be superfluous. The great totalitarian -isms have dreams of a world without something they hate because they think it interferes with their ability to dominate the lives of human beings. Nazism dreamed of a life—of a world without Jews; Communism dreamed of a world without God; and Islamism also dreams of a world without something: it dreams of a world without infidels.

And so we must understand this -ism as well. How do we struggle against Islamism? Obviously, there are limits to how a government like ours can defend itself and the society it governs.

If the First Amendment's establishment clause means anything, it means that our government can't pick winners and losers in doctrinal disputes; that's something the Muslims are going to have to do on their own. But it can take rational steps to defend itself and to avoid irrational steps that undermine its security.

First, those charged with protecting our security have a duty to understand and to teach others under their authority to understand what the basic tenets are of the people who are trying to destroy our way of life. Imagine a president trying to mobilize the country against communism without teaching what communism was about.

Also, those charged with protecting us have a responsibility to avoid strengthening the hand of those who are trying to undermine our way of life by relying on them as our principal interlocutors in the Muslim community. CAIR, the Council on American-Islamic Relations, is a branch of Hamas and of the Muslim Brotherhood. ISNA, the Islamic Society of North America, is another branch of the Muslim Brotherhood. The Muslim Brotherhood traces itself back to Hasan al-Banna and Sayid Qutb. Its motto, which has not changed to this day, is as follows:

Allah is our objective,
the Prophet is our leader,
the Koran is our law,
jihad is our way,
dying in the way of Allah is our highest hope.

If those are the people we empower by relying on them when reaching out to them, we not only damage ourselves by giving them entry into the upper reaches of our political system, but we correspondingly strengthen them in the Islamic community and weaken the reasonable voices, like Dr. Zuhdi Jasser's and others.

Speaking of weakening the reasonable voices like Zuhdi Jasser's, let me give you a glimpse of how people try to do that. Dr. Jasser was invited recently by a group to speak here in New York. And, since one of the group was a member a prominent law firm here in town, that lawyer decided he would host the speech.

The senior manager of diversity development at that firm then received a two page letter on the letterhead of the Muslim Bar Association of New York, date May 8 2012. Now I'm not going to read the whole letter—nor am I going to name the firm—but I think it would be useful for you to hear precisely how this works: The letter begins by announcing the writer's purpose, being "to express concern regarding an event that is taking place at your firm." The event, of course, was Dr. Jasser's speech.

The letter tells us that Mr. Jasser—no reference to either his medical degree and certainly none to his service in the US Navy—is a "controversial figure" who has been "closely linked to Islamophobia" (there's that word again) in the United States. "Many Muslim Americans regard his positions as offensive and troubled."

The letter then goes on to say that this bar association, "has long been aware of this firm's commitment to diversity, inclusion, and tolerance." And it then goes on to recite several examples of diversity, inclusion, and tolerance that were directed at Muslims by this firm.

It then returns to Zuhdi Jasser:

> Despite the moderate facade that he and his American Islamic Forum for Democracy profess, Mr. Jasser has been directly linked to some of the most notorious purveyors of Islamophobia in the United States today. Mr. Jasser is the narrator of The Third Jihad, the anti-Muslim film that was the center of last year's NYPD training controversy. The film, which has been condemned by Muslim organizations and civil rights groups was later characterized as wacky and inappropriate by the NYPD.

The Islamophobes to whom Dr. Jasser is connected include, of course, Andy McCarthy and our host tonight, Frank Gaffney. The Muslim organizations and civil rights groups that have condemned the firm, naturally, are CAIR and ISNA—both Muslim Brotherhood fronts.

So far as the film, I've seen it. It's both balanced and intelligent, making clear that the producer and narrator, Dr. Jasser (himself a Muslim), has nothing against Islam or Muslims. And as for the characterization by the police department, that came at the direction of the mayor, who had not seen the film himself—and whose backbone, to paraphrase Teddy Roosevelt, would be more rigid if it were strapped to a banana.

The letter then goes on for a bit about Dr. Jasser and then comes to its penultimate paragraph:

> To be clear, the Muslim Bar Association fully and unconditionally supports Mr. Jasser's right to speak his mind and the host organization's right

to invite him. We also recognize that law firms like yours regularly lend space to outside organizations for public and private events. As a partner in the mission to promote inclusion and diversity, we solely wanted to make sure you were aware of Mr. Jasser's track record and his stature within the Muslim legal community. Especially in light of the inquiries we have received regarding [your firm]'s role in hosting Mr. Jasser. We are concerned that having such a divisive figure associated with your firm could undermine [your firm]'s image with Muslim attorneys within and outside the firm. Muslim law students considering [your firm] and members of the Muslim community at large.

In other words, as the heavy used to say in old B movies, "you got such a pretty face. Wouldn't it be a shame if something happened to it?"

However, here I have to tell you that this story has a happy ending: that speech was not canceled. It's going to go ahead. But our leaders have a duty not to strengthen the hand of people like the person who wrote that letter. They have a duty to stop using them and their allies as targets of outreach.

In addition, those charged with protecting us have a duty to avoid self-censorship and self-delusion: as you heard Andy McCarthy point out, the after-action report on Major Nidal Hasan's massacre at Fort Hood — which he preceded by shouting *Allahu Akbar*—does not mention the word "Islam." The Army's Chief of Staff said on television after that massacre that the greatest tragedy would be if it had a negative effect on the Army's diversity program.

John Brennan, national security adviser and counter-terrorism adviser to president Obama, told an audience at the Center for Strategic and International Studies—and this is a deep thinker talking to other deep thinkers—that, "violent extremists" attacking the United States are, "products of political, economic, and social forces," and shouldn't be described "in religious terms because to do so would create the mistaken impression that we are at war with Islam and thereby give credence to al-Qaeda propaganda."

"Products of political, economic and social forces"? Let's review the bidding: Osama bin Laden was a millionaire many times over. His successor, and also the folks who planned and carried out the 2007 attack on the Glasgow airport, are physicians. The perpetrators of the 9/11 attack were well-educated university students. Umar Farouk Abdullmutallab, who tried to blow himself up along with his fellow passengers aboard an airplane over Detroit on Christmas Day in 2009, is the son of the former economics minister of Nigeria. "Products of political, economic, and social forces"?

I mention John Brennan not because he's unique, but because he is a perfect symbol of the soft-headed diffidence that has infected the discourse of our public figures. Not that this is new to the point of being unprecedented. It isn't. The smart set in the 1920s ridiculed the values and lifestyle of what they called the bourgeoisie. Anti-anti-communism was fashionable in some circles in the 1950s. And a great liberal judge, Learned Hand—often called the greatest appellate judge ever to sit—said in an address called *The Spirit of Liberty*, "the spirit of liberty is the spirit that is not too sure that it is right." Well, that may be, if not exactly true, at least an affordable indulgence at times. It may even have been an affordable indulgence at the time that Hand said it, which was in the late spring of 1944, when victory against the -ism of that day was, if not exactly around the corner, at least pretty well certain. But today, when we are up against people who are sufficiently sure that they are right to fly airplanes into buildings, we had best make certain that the spirit of liberty is sure enough that it is right and that those responsible for protecting us are sure enough that it is right to keep that spirit—and us—alive.

Thank you again for the honor of this award and the even greater honor of speaking to you.

www.ingramcontent.com/pod-product-compliance
Lightning Source LLC
Chambersburg PA
CBHW020445030426
42337CB00014B/1410